Dedicated to

Mrs. Dianne McDonald

who is used of God as a helper,
encourager, and a friend
to many, many people like me.

Copyright © 1992 by Dennis Corle Evangelistic Assoc.
re-printed 2005
ISBN# 1-932744-13-4

Revival Fires Publishing
P.O. Box 245 • Claysburg, PA 16625
(814) 239-2813

What In The World Should I Wear?

by Mrs. Cathy Corle

Foreword

Early in our ministry, my husband encouraged me to make some message tapes for ladies, and as I'm not a speaker, and probably never will be, it took a lot of talking. Finally I did, and one of the subjects that I dealt with was the subject of ladies' apparel, in a message titled "What In The World Should I Wear?" The Lord had settled this matter in my heart from the Bible, and I simply shared why I believe as I do, that I am responsible to God to dress in a way that is feminine and modest, and exactly what that means in light of the Bible. A number of ladies told me that this message answered their questions and helped them to understand Bible convictions as they never had before.

One of these ladies was Dianne McDonald, and she continually encouraged me to get this message out for more ladies to hear. I guess I was not very convinced that I had anything to say that could not be said better by someone else, but every time I saw her or talked to her Dianne assured me that many ladies would be helped and I needed to do something more with this material. But with a busy on-the-road schedule, motherhood, school and a monthly newspaper deadline, I couldn't seem to get it done.

Several months ago, the Lord really convicted my heart for several ladies I know, as well as several churches, where this issue had caused a major problem --- perhaps needlessly. I told the Lord I didn't know if I could help or not, but I'd do my little part. So for the next four months I ran a series of articles in *Revival Fires!* that consisted of the same material I had studied years ago that had made my decision for me. I asked the Lord to help me, did the best I could, and sent it out.

The response has been amazing. With each article many people wrote and asked for more copies, some asked for permission to reprint the article for the ladies in their churches. Ladies wrote. Men wrote. Preachers wrote. Parents wrote. People called on the phone. I could not believe how many people said it was just what was needed in their church, their family, or their own life.

Countless people have requested this material in the form of a booklet, so here it is. I hope it's a help to you, as it has been to me, and I guess to others also. But if it is, don't thank me, because I probably would have never done it on my own. You can say thanks to a lovely lady who knows how to encourage people to go on with what they probably already know God wants them to do, but don't have the confidence to do it. Thank you, Dianne.

What In The World Should I Wear?

Part One

Have you ever said that on an occasion? I know that I have. I want you, for a little while, to take that statement literally and ask yourself, "What - in the world - *should* - I - wear?" What kind of clothing is available in the world that is appropriate for me, as a Christian who wants to please God, to wear as a good testimony in my appearance? What kind of clothing will bring glory to God through my very presence among people?

I want you to stop right now and promise the Lord that as you learn what He wants you to wear, you will do just that. I am not asking you to wear what I tell you is right or proper, but I AM challenging you to promise the Lord that what you can see clearly from His Word you will instantly apply to your own wardrobe. Promise Him that as you understand what He has in mind for the way that you clothe your body, that you will not disobey Him. We as ladies need God's help in the area of our appearance, because His Word says that we are 'living epistles' and that unsaved people are looking at us to determine their opinion of Christianity. That causes us to realize that how we look on the outside is so very important, and is closely linked to what we are on the inside.

This message is not given in a spirit of criticism and malice, but in an attempt of love and helpfulness to ladies who are concerned. We need definite guidance that is not a set of man-made rules and preferences, but a standard that comes straight from the Bible that defines how God chooses for ladies to be dressed.

For those who have the attitude, "I like the kind of clothes that I already have, and I'm not going to change for anybody - not even the Lord", this will not be any help at all. But I know that there are ladies in the same predicament that I once found myself, who want to do right but aren't quite sure what that means in the area of apparel.

I had the attitude, "I'm not going to change for every different person that comes to town with a different idea than the last guy about what's right to wear. But if I knew exactly what the Lord wanted, I would do it without a second thought in order to please Him." Many people told me things I should and shouldn't wear, but no one gave me a scriptural basis for it that could stand up against my questions, so I had little confidence in what they said. The problem was not that they had the wrong standards, as I learned later, but that they had 'inherited' standards that they had just accepted from someone else. They had never found out why and where it was in the scripture and what God had to say concerning proper dress.

For those ladies with a sincere desire to do right, and those who are already doing right on 'inherited' convictions, I think this message can be a real assistance in helping them to formulate, right out of the scriptures, a definite guideline for ladies' dress. Let the Lord answer your questions today, so you, too, will know the answer to: "What In The World Should I

Wear?"

What In The World Is This All About?

The Bible has alot to say about the world and worldliness in the life of a Christian. First Corinthians 7:31 says, *"And they that use this world, as not abusing it: for the fashion of this world passeth away."* Here we have a basic guideline we can apply to dress standards. It says in essence that it is not wrong to use the world - it is wrong to abuse the world. Just because a dress is becoming and in style does not make it wrong. Being attractive does not violate Bible principle, but rather we should be dressed attractively in a manner that shows the world our femininity - not our sexuality.

Some people have the false notion that anything pretty is wrong, women should wear dark baggy clothing, wear their hair in a bun and no makeup so that they don't draw any attention. But God didn't make women to be ugly! Woman was His crowning act of creation that He intended to be even more beautiful than the breathtaking scenery of creation or the lovely works of nature made by His own hand.

So I want ladies to know right from the start that our purpose in dress standards is not to make ladies look dowdy and unattractive, but just the opposite. If a certain type of garment is in style, you cannot assume that makes it automatically right or automatically wrong. You need to examine it in light of a scriptural check-list that we will be compiling right now. It is not wrong to use the world, when there is something available that also measures up to the Bible's standard of apparel. It is wrong to abuse the world, wearing clothes just because it's the style of the day, even though it violates the Word of God and harms our testimony before the world.

That the *'fashion of this world passeth away'*, we know full well. The styles change so quickly and clothing that was called an 'absolute must' last year is outdated now. Five or ten years ago we laughed at pictures of our mothers and vowed we would never be seen in some of the exact things we are wearing today. No doubt our daughters will see the same merry-go-round of dress styles in their life-time, if the Lord tarries. But as the 'last days' are in full-swing, and the devil has an ever-strengthening grip on the world in general, and the world of fashion in particular, there is less and less available at the store down the street that meets God's approval in the way of women's wear.

This was a problem even in Charles Spurgeon's day. In one sermon he announced, "London gets their fashions straight from Paris, and Paris gets their fashions straight from Hell." He was stating more truth than we might realize. The Bible says some very distinct and plain things concerning worldliness. When a woman dresses in a manner that flaunts her sexuality or promotes a Unisex image, we hear preachers refer to her clothing as 'worldly'. Worldliness is almost always referring to sins of separation -- participation in these practices identified with the world.

Scripture defines 'the world' not as the globe, but

as the kingdom order set up by Satan when he gained dominion of it. Second Corinthians 4:4 identifies Satan as *'the god of this world'.* So the world is the kingdom that Satan has set up to fulfill his own purposes and practices, to meet his goals. Worldliness is conforming to the desires of the god of this world in the same measure that Christianity is conforming to the desires of God in Heaven.   Isaiah 14:12-14 defines Satan's goals: he wished to make himself equal with God, to overthrow the worship of God and win worship to himself, to rule and reign over all creation in the place of God.

Why is it that godly preachers cry out against worldliness? It's because worldliness gives the glory to sin and to Satan which rightfully belongs to God and righteousness. Why are most movies worldly? Because they glorify sin of all kinds and present it as the devil wants sin to be viewed so that sin is no more 'exceedingly sinful' to us, and we become accustomed to its presence. Why are rock music and country music considered worldly? Because they incessantly indoctrinate the listener with tales of wickedness that become a part of his subconscious thinking and decision-making. Examine the issues, and you will realize that worldliness is participation in Satan's kingdom, allowing him to be glorified and set up in the place of pre-eminence in our lives.

Worldliness, therefore, is an act of bringing glory to Satan's kingdom in the same measure that godliness brings glory to the kingdom of God. Worldliness promotes sin just as godliness promotes righteousness. You say, "I'm not a bad person because of what I wear. I'm just not a fanatic." The Bible is plain, however, that there is no middle ground in any area of our life. *"He that is not with me is against me."* -- *"Know ye not that the friendship of the world is enmity with God? Whosoever therefore will be a friend of the world is the enemy of God."* (*James 4:4*) To refuse God's standard of apparel is to choose one that will promote sin and bring glory to Satan. The devil has a whole line of women's wear designed specifically to promote sensuality, promiscuity, homosexuality and a host of other vile practices. So Spurgeon really was stating fact in saying that Paris gets their fashions straight from Hell!

We are given some stern commands concerning our relationship to this world that reflect the danger that it presents to our spiritual lives. *"Love not the world, neither the things that are in the world. If any man love the world, the love of the Father is not in him. For all that is in the world, the lust of the flesh, and the lust of the eyes, and the pride of life, is not of the Father, but is of the world. And the world passeth away, and the lust thereof; but he that doeth the will of God abideth for ever."* (*1John 2:15-17*) God wasn't telling us not to love the globe, or not to appreciate this earthly masterpiece. He was telling us not to love Satan's empire here and all that it stands for. I know ladies who would give up God before they would give up their unChristian wardrobe. They love the devil's world more than they love the Lord.

Again in Romans 12:2 we are given instruction

concerning the world. *"And be not conformed to this world: but be ye transformed by the renewing of your mind, that ye may prove what is that good, and acceptable, and perfect, will of God."* We are not supposed to strive to fit in and seem acceptable to the world's way of life. The devil is sure to try squeezing us into his mold so that we'll conform. God gives us the alternative of allowing Him to transform us into the image of Christ in the same kind of metamorphosis that miraculously makes a caterpillar become a butterfly. But I can't be both. I must first shun the temptation to conform for the devil before I can be transformed for the glory of Christ.

Worldliness damages our testimony, is a reproach to the Gospel of Christ, sears our conscience to the Holy Spirit's working, and puts up a wall of separation that prohibits fellowship with God and getting prayers answered. Worldliness is not an unimportant matter that we can afford to ignore.

What In The World Should I Wear? Join us for part two, as we continue with The Divine Dress Code, right out of the Bible.

What In The World Should I Wear?

Part Two

The Divine Dress Code

"In like manner also, that women adorn themselves in modest apparel, with shame-facedness and sobriety; not with broided hair, or gold, or pearls, or costly array; But (which becometh women professing godliness) with good works." (1Timothy 2:9-10) Modest apparel, in this passage, is not referring to a characteristic about clothing, but is referring to a specific type of garment. *Katastole* is the Greek word which is translated 'modest apparel'. The literal definition of the word is 'a long flowing garment that is let down'. This is the primary yardstick by which we are to measure our wardrobe. The scriptural dress-code for a lady, then, is a garment that is long and loose-fitting, so as not to reveal the feminine contours of a woman's body intended only for her husband's eyes. So what kind of clothing does this include?

First of all it does not include pants or slacks as feminine wear. Some schools and churches permit girls to wear pants for sports and activities by saying that they are more modest than a dress or culottes, but there is nothing modest about a pair of pants. There is no possible way you could stretch this scriptural rule of a 'long flowing garment' to include pants. Although they may qualify as long, pants don't flow -- they squeak!   Some people insist on calling them slacks when there is no slack in them.   A woman's body is not at all concealed by wearing pants and jeans, it is simply displayed in a different color. All of the anatomy that would be discreetly covered by a KATASTOLE, namely the thighs, crotch and derriere, is only more emphasized by slacks.

A friend of mine told me that her decision to restrict her wardrobe to dresses and skirts came as a result of a ladies' class. All the arguments and reasons that could be given were unheeded until the lady who was speaking said, "Let me just demonstrate something to you." She asked the ladies in the audience to close their eyes momentarily. She held up a large picture of a woman in an attractive, feminine skirt and blouse. She asked the ladies to open their eyes. Then she inquired, "What is the primary focal point to this picture? Where did your eyes first fall naturally?" The audience agreed that their eyes were first drawn to the face of the woman in the picture.

She once again asked the ladies to close their eyes. When they opened their eyes they were looking at a large poster of a woman in a sport shirt and blue jeans. She asked, "Now, be honest with yourselves, and tell me where your eyes first fell naturally when you looked at this picture?" Many of the ladies in the crowd were surprised to find that most people's eyes first focused upon the hips and crotch area that were so vividly emphasized before they ever noticed the woman's face. If this happened in a crowd of ladies, how much more would it be true of men? For my friend, Joetta, this was all the 'evidence' that was needed.   Pants are mentioned in the Bible several times and are called 'breeches'. They are NEVER identified or associated with a woman's apparel. Speaking of the priests' garments, the Bible says, *"And thou shalt make them linen breeches to cover their nakedness; from the loins even unto the thighs they shall reach: And they shall be upon Aaron, and upon his sons, when they come in unto the tabernacle..."* *(Exodus 28:42-43)*   You will only find britches or pants as a masculine garment.

Deuteronomy 22:5 says, *"A woman shall not wear that which pertaineth to a man, neither shall a man put on a woman's garment: for all that do so are an ABOMINATION to the Lord thy God."* Webster's Dictionary defines an abomination as "a disgusting, hateful, or loathsome thing."   The most heinous deeds imaginable are categorized in scripture as being an abomination, such as homosexuality, bestiality, mock worship that ridicules the Lord, witchcraft, and other serious offenses. God says that He is just that disgusted and sickened by women who wear men's garments. But who says that pants are a man's garment? God did! Contrary to what we have been led to believe by art, television, etc. men's and women's apparel in Bible times were not identical. There was a very plain distinction between the clothing of each.

The major difference between the masculine outfit then and now is that those men wore a longer robe or upper garment than the shirt or jacket usually worn by men today. In some eras, they were knee-length, but much of the time they were even longer. With this *STOLE*, the man's apparel included breeches and a special kind of belt that was called a girdle. When a man was not engaged in active pursuits, this outer garment was left hanging loose for coolness and comfort.

When he began manual labor or some strenuous activity he would gather up the lower portion of this robe and tuck it into the girdle which was worn especially for that purpose. This freed his legs from interference as he worked. He was still sufficiently clothed when he did so because he wore breeches or pants under his outer robe. According to the verse we've already quoted, these breeches were always at least long enough to cover the leg down to the knee.

Hence, we have the phrase, **'Gird up your loins'**, which is mentioned in the Bible concerning men. The Lord commanded Job twice to gird up his loins and specified it as a masculine dress practice. Job 38:3 *"Gird up now thy loins LIKE A MAN; for I will demand of thee, and answer thou me."* Job 40:7 *"Gird up thy loins now LIKE A MAN: I will demand of thee, and declare thou unto me."*

This phrase is never used concerning a woman, nor any other reference that would suggest pants as part of a woman's apparel. The practice of wearing breeches and a short upper garment, or of pulling up that upper garment to expose the legs and thighs in pants is ONLY ever practiced or approved of for men, as far as the Bible is concerned.

The following is from Zondervan's Pictorial

Dictionary: "A few articles of female clothing carried somewhat the same name and same basic pattern as a man's, yet there was always sufficient difference... so that in appearance, the line of demarcation between men and women could readily be detected." I am told that even from a distance, it was readily apparent whether a person in view was a man or a woman. We are making a lame excuse when we say that it is acceptable for women to dress as men and men as women because we think that they did so in Bible times. This is simply not true.

I am sure that you have heard of the rock and roll personality, 'Boy George'. He is a rock star that wears women's clothing, make-up, hair-style, and looks and sounds like a female when he performs. He explained that he found it necessary to label himself 'Boy George' so that people would know that he was male. One fan publication called him "The Gender Blender Of The Eighties". God never intended for there to be a gender blender, and this is made plain by many Bible passages. The Lord put specific difference between men and women in clothing and hair length so that a person could be immediately identified by their silhouette as either a man or a woman, and gave direct command that we maintain these distinctions. People like Boy George are displaying their rebellion against the Lord in blatantly crossing these boundaries. This is an abomination to God. *"...Neither shall a man put on a woman's garment, for all that do so are an abomination to the Lord thy God."*

The following letter was written to advice

columnist Ann Landers:

"Dear Ann, Your column does a world of good. You touched on a topic recently that helped me tremendously. I am one of those men who likes to dress in women's clothes. Shortly before you printed the letter signed 'Bobette's Wife', my wife discovered my private cachet of ladies' wear. She became hysterical, accused me of being a homosexual, and made an appointment to see a lawyer about a divorce. After she read your column she cancelled her appointment with the lawyer and made an appointment with the doctor. She took your column along. The doctor said that you were right, that most transvestites are not homosexuals. They enjoy dressing in female attire, but have no desire to engage in homosexual activities. Some homosexuals are, however, transvestites, and that causes the confusion. Knowing full well that I cannot curb my desires, my wife now leaves the house one evening a week while I 'play lady'. I prefer to be alone and unobserved and she respects my wishes. I always make sure that the children are asleep, I draw the draperies and do not answer the doorbell. Since I've been able to carry out my little charade with my wife's knowledge and approval I feel 100% better. My nerves are settled and I'm off tranquilizers. Thank you for being broad-minded. --Ann's Fan"

You are probably responding the same way I did. "Ugh--gross!" We cannot imagine a man so perverted and deranged as to get a charge out of parading around in negligees and lace panties. We can't imagine our husbands or acquaintances ever entertaining such thoughts and just the idea horrifies us. It seems very logical to us that God's feelings about the subject should be just as vehement as our own. *"...Neither shall a man put on a woman's garment; for all that do so are an ABOMINATION to the Lord thy God."* It makes all the sense in the world to us to think that this would make God sick.

But wait, what is it that tells you that men shouldn't wear dresses and negligees? How do you know that they are solely meant for women? I believe that we know in the same way that the Scripture says we know about hair length - that nature itself teaches us. God programmed into us the instinctive knowledge that dresses or *KATASTOLES* are women's apparel and men shouldn't wear them. We agree with God that such a practice deserves to be considered as an abomination.

Follow your train of thought for a few moments, though. Why is it that a man should not wear a dress? Because it is a woman's apparel? If a man is not supposed to wear a dress, what is he supposed to wear? Pants? Does that mean, then, that pants are a man's apparel? If a dress is specifically a woman's garment, what garment belongs to and characterizes manhood in this culture?

I've seen men in skirts before --- and I'm sure I'll never get used to it. But we fail to remember that 75 years ago people were just as shocked to see a woman in pants as we are today to see a man in a skirt. It was just as common to assume that women wearing pants were as unnatural and out of line as men in dresses. By continual exposure, the devil can cause us to accept any kind of sin, and this is the hidden danger of television.

In this generation we have grown so accustomed to seeing women wear pants that it no longer seems out of place, and most women in the 1990's have worn pants all of their lives. We live in a generation where some girls have never actually owned a dress. And yet God hasn't changed. *"A woman shall not wear that which pertaineth to a man...for all that do so are an abomination to the Lord thy God."* God still has the same hatred for women wearing men's clothing that He had when the Bible was written.

Skirts for men are being railroaded through the fashion marketplace, and it may not be too many years in the future that they will be just as commonplace and acceptable to us as pants for women. On his nationally acclaimed talk show, host Phil Donahue interviewed fashion designers concerning the up and coming trend of men's skirts. Several male models were wearing skirts, as was Mr. Donahue himself. When the conversation was opened for comment from the audience, the women were quick to voice their dismay and disapproval at such an offensive practice. Donahue turned to them and said, "If it is wrong for men to wear skirts, then it is equally wrong for you women to wear pants." Just like the skillet calling the kettle black, women who insist that men ought not wear feminine clothing are day-after-day wearing masculine attire.

The command of clothing distinction is stated even more specifically and stringently for women than it is for men. Men are simply not to wear women's garments. God said that a woman is not to wear that which pertaineth to a man, anything that resembles or reminds one of a man's clothing. It is not the clothes themselves that are abominable to God, it is the people who wear them - *'all that do so are an abomination'*. When the Bible uses the word 'abomination' it is a serious offense. Certainly this is not a minor issue.

Continue with us into part three as we look a little further about where our dress standards are defined in scripture. I hope that you're sincere and submissive about looking into God's word for the answer to this question: "What in the world should I wear?"

ᴡ̓hat In The ᴡ̓orld Should I ᴡ̓ear?

Part Three

I hope that you've been reading along with us during the past two months as we've been exploring the Bible concerning godly dress standards for ladies. First we talked about the meaning of worldiness, which is the opposite of godliness. Worldiness is any practice that glorifies sin and self and furthers the devil's plans for our lives just as godliness brings glory to Christ, exalts holy living and expresses submission to God's plan for our lives. Worldly attire, then, is any clothing that does not glorify God through my appearance, but points rather to sensuality or rebellion against God's plan and distinction between men and women.

In last month's column, we examined Deuteronomy 22:5 and I Timothy 2:9 which teach clearly that proper apparel for women consists of 'a long flowing garment, which is let down'. Only men were ever expected to 'gird up their loins', exposing their legs and lower body covered by breeches. A woman's garment is always to be let down, and breeches never have been part of the wardrobe that God intended for women to wear.

I began to wonder, "Why is this such an explosive issue?" I've seen preachers preach against rock music, and people brought their tapes and albums and burned them. I've heard preachers preach against alcohol, pornography, soap operas, and all kinds of vile sin, and never heard anybody try to justify it. But just let the preacher preach against women wearing pants and shorts and halter tops and bathing suits and mini-skirts, and suddenly you have a world war going on. Churches have been split, friendships have been severed, the work of Christ has been damaged because so many women insist on claiming something is right that God says is wrong. Why is that?

Effeminate men, masculine women, transvestism and homosexuality are certainly more common today than at any time since Sodom and Gomorrah. But I've yet to hear of a problem in Bible preaching churches over saved men who insist on wearing women's clothing. I've never heard an invitation for men to come forward and give up their skirts, have you? This issue is not a real problem for the men in our churches. Yet women who have refused to part with their masculine pants have been responsible for scores of church splits and thousands of women have moved their membership to First Compromiser Church or quit church altogether because pants or slacks or breeches have such a hold on their hearts.

The same women who wouldn't rebel over preaching on any other subject will have a hysterical fit when the preacher gets up and says that Deuteronomy 22:5 says that women ought not to wear men's clothes. Clearly, the devil has a real strong-hold or foot-hold in the lives of women in this area. Separation in our dress standards will stir up trouble in a church like little else can. Again --- why is this so volatile a topic?

In studying the subject a few years ago and examining more closely what the Bible has to say about this, it became evident to me. When God gave the distinctions between men and women in dress and in hair length, he chose for the lady to wear a dress -- a long flowing garment -- and hair that is long and flowing, which is more gracious and feminine and lovely than the appearance of a man. God directed for a man to wear pants or breeches and a short hair-cut, which by nature is more masculine.

The Bible is clear that we instinctively know that this is proper and natural, unless of course we've allowed ourselves to be programmed against the natural inclinations that God has placed within us. *"Doth not even nature itself teach you, that, if a man have long hair, it is a shame unto him? But if a woman have long hair, it is a glory to her: for her hair is given her for a covering."* (I Corinthians 11:14) Nature tells us that a man ought to have short hair, and of course a woman's hair-style ought to be the opposite, and ought to be easily distinguished from a man's.

The distinctions that God described between a man and a woman ought to point out plainly the difference in the office or position that God intended for them in His chain of command. *"But I would have you know, that the head of every man is Christ; and the head of the woman is the man; and the head of Christ is God."* (I Corinthians 11:3) Just as short hair speaks of the man's position and responsibility, pants, being identified as male attire, have also become a symbol of the man's authority.

The chain of command was a much less important detail in God's original scheme of things. When there was no sin, there was no danger of clashing wills or conflicting directions. But immediately, when sin came into the world, the necessity for authority and follow-ship came with it. Immediately after the fall, in Genesis 3:16, God set the pattern. *"Unto the woman he said, I will greatly multiply thy sorrow and thy conception; in sorrow thou shalt bring forth children; and thy desire shall be to thy husband, and HE SHALL RULE OVER THEE."*

Dr. Charles Keen, in a message on the home, said something like this: "I like for my children to wonder sometimes who is in charge at our house. Now, they know that Dad is the authority, and that Mom is under his leadership. But when both partners are truly Spirit-filled, and operating in love and consideration for one another, there is seldom a need for this to be demonstrated. Perfect oneness, like God intended for marriage, needs no chain of command, but as sinners, we must have this God-given rule for authority in our homes. When our purpose and desire is one, there is little outward expression of one ruling and the other submitting. That's the kind of loving atmosphere I want to see in my home."

With sin came the need for authority and submission, and the Bible is plain that the feminine length of a lady's hair is an outward display of her inward surrender to her husband's authority. Immediately after these verses, the Bible goes on to say, *"For this cause* (because of the differing offices of man and woman in marriage) *ought the woman to*

have power on her head because of the angels...
Doth not even nature itself teach you, that, if a
man have long hair, it is a shame unto him? But
if a woman have long hair, it is a glory to her: for
her hair is given her for a covering." (I
Corinthians 11:10, 14, 15)   The word for 'power'
means 'jurisdiction', the privilege or right to rule.
Hence a woman's long hair is signifying her husband's
right to be her authority.

When it says that a woman's hair is given to her
for a 'covering', that is the same word used for 'veil'.
This gives us some specific guidelines as to how long a
woman's hair should be. "How short is short and how
long is long?" I know you've heard that question
before! A woman's hair ought to be long enough to be
considered a veil, or have length that covers. When a
person's hair grows beyond the natural hairline, what
is the first thing it covers? The ears and the neck, of
course. In order to pass the test of I Corinthians 11, a
woman's hair ought to have enough length to hang
down and cover the ears and neck, and a man's hair
ought to be short enough that it does not hang on the
neck and ears.

God said that a woman ought to have long hair,
first of all, as an outward symbol of her voluntary
submission to her husband. Secondly, He said it was
because of the angels. So, it may not seem very
important to other people, but God says that in the
spiritual realm it is very important, and that it is
noticed by spiritual beings. Should we conclude, then,
that not only the angels, but also God and Satan take
note of a woman's hair length and the meaning behind

it?

Let's look back at I Timothy 2 again. *"In like manner also, that women adorn themselves in modest apparel, with shamefacedness and sobriety; ... Let the woman learn in silence with all subjection. But I suffer not a woman to teach, nor to usurp authority over the man, but to be in silence. For Adam was first formed, then Eve. And Adam was not deceived, but the woman being deceived was in the transgression."* (verses 9, 11-14) Just as God showed us the correlation between a woman's hair and her willing submission to God-given authority, He once again shows the relation between a woman wearing modest apparel outwardly and submitting to her husband inwardly. Directly after the command for a woman to be dressed in a long flowing garment, the chain of command is outlined again. Not only our hair, but also our dress, is an outward sign of our inward submission to God and to our husbands.

In part two, through the letter written to Ann Landers from a transvestite, I demonstrated to you what is our natural response for a man to wear dresses or lacy, feminine attire. Nobody ever sat us down and drilled us, "This is wrong! This is wrong!" Nobody had to. We already know it's wrong. Just as *'nature itself teaches us'* about the hair lengths of men and women, nature also teaches us that it is wrong for a man to wear a dress, and equally wrong for a woman to wear pants.

The Bible shows the correlation between a woman's submission or rebellion and what she wears.

Pants have always been a symbol of the man, and the man's authority. When you look for a public restroom, you'll often find two doors with no words. One sign has a figure dressed in a skirt, the sign on the other door has a figure dressed in pants. Does that cause you to stand out in the hallway and wonder which one is which? No! We already know, because pants have always been associated with men. Even the world knows that. If we took those signs seriously, we would really need only one restroom, because nearly everybody is dressed in pants nowadays. (It's becoming all too common that you find only one restroom for both men and ladies to use!)

You've heard people say it for years: "There's no question about who wears the pants in that family." Pants are a symbol of a man's authority, and when a woman wears them, she is displaying on her body a message about what's in her heart. Mrs. Libby Handford made a power-packed statement in that one sentence which titles her book: "Your Clothes Say It For You." Your clothes say a lot about you, and most of the people who see you everyday don't stop to talk with you, but they can clearly read the message you convey by the way that you dress.

So what do your pants say about you? "I'm my own boss. I'm taking the reins and my husband or my parents have no right to tell me what to do. I refuse to obey my God-given authority." Rebellion, plain and simple. The first sin in history was rebellion. Satan exalted himself against God and fell from his lofty position in heaven. Every sin that has ever been committed came from that one. The first sin of mankind was also rooted in rebellion. The devil promised Eve, "Ye shall be as gods, knowing good and evil." Part of the temptation that Eve fell prey to was the desire to be like God, not in holiness, but in power and authority. Satan encouraged Eve to share in the sin of rebellion, and he encourages us in the same direction. I never began to understand why the sin of women wearing men's apparel was classified as an abomination, with the most horrid and heinous acts imaginable. Not until I realized that the sin of rebellion was at the very root of the matter.

According to all that we've examined from the Bible, women wearing pants are a clear symbol of rebellion. No wonder this favored fashion has become such a powerful tool for the devil to use. Notice too, that they haven't become outdated like all the other styles of clothing have made the rounds. Pants for women are one of the all-time favored selections of 'worldly clothing' that the god of this world would like us to wear, since they clearly signify his favorite sin --- rebellion.

Lots of ladies are quick to remind the preacher that *"..man looketh on the outward appearance, but God looketh on the heart."* Well, it's true. A person who covers up on the outside by dressing right when their heart is filled with wickedness cannot fool God. God DOES look on the heart, but that doesn't mean that He's blind to our outward appearance. The Bible is clear that our appearance IS important, else these verses would not be found within its pages. Also, don't forget that "man looketh on the outward appearance." People cannot look upon our hearts to know what's within. They must discern from what we display on the outside.

When you see a fat bird with a large orange bill waddling toward the pond, do you catch it and butcher it before you can decide what type of animal it may be? No, you don't. You say, "There goes a duck." Now how could you gather so much information without seeing what is within? Could it be that God made just about everything so that what it really is inside is clearly identified by what shows on the outside?

A book is known by its cover. Whatever is written on the outside gives you the general idea of what you'll find within its pages. Nobody would print the title "Cookbook" on the cover of a book filled with house plans. Even so, what is inside our heart is clearly displayed on the outside by our actions, our attitudes, our aspirations, and yes, our apparel. If your clothes say it for you, then what are your clothes telling the world about you?

What In The World Should I Wear?

Part Four

How quickly people forget. When you talk about Bible standards of dress, most people look at you like they've never heard of anything of the sort. Yet I remember during my early years at public school that when you went shopping for school clothes, that meant dresses and skirts. I was in the 5th grade before female students and teachers were permitted to wear slacks to school. At the bank across the street, the female employees were required to wear dresses to work, as it was in most stores and businesses.

Pardon me, but I'm really not that old! This has only been a little over 20 years ago! That was the world, the churches, and everybody in between. But when you mention that to someone now, they look at you like you're referring to the dark ages. How is it that in 20 years we've gone from the point where all women wore dresses and skirts in public to where many girls who are my age and younger don't even own a dress?

Is it only coincidence that during that same time period the divorce rate has climbed to 1 out of 2 marriages, and at some points during that time line there have actually been more divorces than marriages taking place? It's not by accident that during these 20 years we have experienced the greatest breakdown in the home and traditional, scriptural roles for husbands and wives, which has affected even Christian families. Now there are even women who have a career while their husbands play "Mr. Mom" and stay home with the kids. Most families, however, consist of two adults who work at separate jobs, lead separate lives, and leave the children to the care of others or to take care of themselves.

In the same measure that women have displayed the authority by 'wearing the pants in the family', they've also usurped the authority and caused this major breakdown. We're now in a second generation where many grown men were raised in homes where mama wore the pants in the family -- not just in apparel, but in authority, as well. You might not think that is a matter of much importance, but according to Biblical standards, that ought to cause a declaration of national disaster!

We've covered some types of clothing that are not right, but what about finding out what is right. If you're like me, despite your desire to do right in the area of dress, there are still some questions you don't have answers for. One of my questions as I approached this subject in my own life years ago was this: If we are expected to wear what women wore in the Bible, why don't we have to wear floor length dresses? Why is it acceptable to wear dresses to the knee?

First Timothy 2:9, the basis for this scriptural 'dress code', says that a woman is to wear modest apparel, a *katastole* or long flowing garment. That makes a further distinction I want to point out --

LONG. Again someone will say, "How long is long, and how short is short?" The world is not worried about being too worldly, but it seems that 'Christians' are trying not be be too Christian. Why do we want to wear what the world wears and convince ourselves that it meets God's approval? The world calls shorts short, they call a mini-skirt mini, and somehow we think we can stretch that to mean long. Does the Bible define 'how long is long'? Is there a specific statement about the length of a *katastole*?

Babylon is called in the book of Revelation the 'mother of harlots'. Isaiah 47, in the first few verses, outlines how Babylon left her virginity and became a harlot. I realize that this is talking about a nation or an empire, but I believe that it has important teaching for literal women, as well.

"Come down, and sit in the dust, O virgin daughter of Babylon, sit on the ground: there is no throne, O daughter of the Chaldeans: for thou shalt no more be called tender and delicate. Take the millstones, and grind meal: uncover thy locks, make bare the leg, uncover the thigh, pass over the rivers. Thy nakedness shall be uncovered, yea, thy shame shall be seen: . . . Sit thou silent, and get thee into darkness, O daughter of the Chaldeans: for thou shalt no more be called, The lady of kingdoms." (Isaiah 47:1-5)

Notice first that she left her royal position to sit in the dust. She lost the charm of innocence and purity. When she left all this behind she was put to work at taxing physical labor. She cut her hair. Most important for us to see here is that she exposed her leg, and specifically the thigh. Here we see that in the progression from being a virgin to becoming a harlot, she bared her thigh. The next statement is, "Pass over the rivers." I would think that this means that she crossed over natural, God-given boundaries. In uncovering the leg and exposing her thigh, the Bible says, *'Thy nakedness shall be uncovered, yea, thy shame shall be seen:"* It goes on to say that she will no longer be regarded as a lady.

There are some powerful things in this passage. The main thing I want to point out is that God equates exposing the thigh with nakedness. If someone suggested that a woman could go to the store naked, we'd be horrified. But many women who are saved think that it's okay as long as you're just 75% or 80% naked. It must be that we don't want to appear dressed in a manner that would be offensive to the world, yet we really aren't concerned about whether God approves or not.

Nakedness includes the uncovering of the thighs, so a long flowing garment that passes God's test for 'modest apparel' MUST cover a woman's body and legs at least to the knee. And, I might add, it must cover the thighs all of the time, while standing, sitting, walking, bending, and everything else that you do. You won't find a skirt or dress that barely brushes the top of the knee-cap that modestly covers a woman all of the time. It's going to have to have some extra length in order to allow for real life, and still cover a woman modestly.

The Bible speaks about the 'attire of an harlot'.

"And, behold, there met him a woman with the attire of an harlot, and subtil of heart." (Proverbs 7:10) Have you stopped to consider what kind of clothing that might have been? What was it that showed a woman's immorality so that it was readily evident to men that she was 'available'?

A woman could not go out in public in clothing that was short enough to reveal the body. But a harlot would display her body by having slits in the skirt to reveal her legs as she walked. To display her legs before men was like 'advertisement'. There was no question in a man's mind about the attire or 'uniform' of a harlot. We've seen the trend of split skirts in our lifetime, but it's not a new style. In this age where most every style of clothing that is popular fits in with the harlot's 'advertisement' of centuries ago, it is no surprise to find out that only a small percentage of young ladies from the local public high school maintain sexual purity all the way to a wedding altar.

If 'modest apparel' means a *katastole* or long flowing garment that completely covers the thigh, then it doesn't mean shorts. Nor does it mean mini-skirts. And it definitely does not mean bathing suits. "But I wear a modest one-piece bathing suit." The fact that your belly-button isn't showing doesn't make it modest. There is no such thing as a modest one-piece bathing suit, unless it covers from your neck to your knees, and is loose and flowing. I've never heard of one of those, have you?

If you wouldn't lay out in your back yard in nothing at all, then you shouldn't lay out in your back yard in a bathing suit either. Let me quote the preaching of my husband, who often says, "Would you mind explaining why you need to tan all that flesh that you're not planning to show?" If you were planning to dress modestly, then you could dress modestly while you're out in the sun also, and everything that ought to show would be tan, right? If American women were half as concerned about their character, their walk with God, their marriage or their children as they are about their tan, America wouldn't be in this shape! I know you're hoping I'll get off that subject, so let's go on.

Women are to dress modestly. I dare you to check your Bible out sometime in July and see if it doesn't say the same thing that it says in December. The Bible doesn't change seasonally with your wardrobe. It doesn't change with the location, either. It says the same thing in Miami, Florida that it says if you read it in Alaska. "But it's hot outside." I reckon it used to get hot back when God said that women should be dressed in modest apparel, too.

I've heard my husband say, "I'm not against mixed swimming, I'm against mixed nudity." The problem is not the water or the sport, it's the lack of clothing. At our Christian camps we have the opportunity for girls to have a private swimming time, and then boys. The world doesn't do us that favor, though. There may sometimes be opportunities when your family can swim or play in the water and everyone be dressed in their normal clothes, providing that they don't become 'transparent' or revealing when they are wet. But even though you are dressed modestly, remember that you never should expose yourself or your husband or your children to an atmosphere where other people are displaying their nudity. (If you take your husband to the beach or the pool to look at all the other women in bikinis and swimsuits, you've got an extra hole in your head!)

Pastor Bruce Goddard presented the issue of modesty in a sermon like this. "If a lady was scheduled to sing a special up here on the platform, and she came up dressed only in underclothing, everyone here would be outraged. But suppose she was going to come up on the platform of the church to sing a special in only underclothing, but she decided that first she'd paint some flowers or stripes on it to make it acceptable. Would that make it right? But what if we shipped in a truck load of sand, and a palm tree, and some beautiful water that she could be surrounded by while she sang an old hymn of the faith dressed in only underclothing that was decorated with flowers? Now it would be all right, wouldn't it? What if we transferred her out to the beach with the sand and the palm trees and the ocean, would it be any more right for her to represent the Lord and sing about Him dressed only in underclothing that was decorated with flowers? If it would not be right to sing hymns dressed in that fashion, then it is not right to do anything dressed -- or undressed -- in that way. Our job is to represent the Lord all the time."

Many women who wouldn't dare to answer the door in their underclothing have no problem with going out in the yard or out on the beach in a bathing suit that covers about the same thing, or less. Since it's acceptable to the world, and many of us only care about pleasing the world, then we do as they do and could care less that God says it is nakedness.

If Babylon crossed over God-given boundaries when she uncovered the thigh and bared the leg for public viewing, then God has a boundary or standard of modesty for us, as well. The Bible draws the line at knee-length for a garment to pass God's test for modest apparel.

You may be surprised to learn that it is not only God, and the Bible, and old-fashioned preachers who think that a woman who exposes her thighs is immodest. Mary Quant, the designer of the mini-skirt, said this: "Am I the only woman who ever wanted to go to bed with a man in the afternoon? Any law-abiding female used to think that she had to wait until after dark. Well, there's just a lot of us girls who don't want to wait until night. I made it so that a man can look at you and say, 'There's a girl from whom I can get anything I want. The dress tells me so.'" The mini-skirt was introduced 20 years ago and made history as the trademark of the sexual revolution. The world agrees that to expose the thigh is to invite immorality.

The Bible says that if a man looks on a woman to lust after her, he has already committed adultery in his heart. But when a woman invites such attention and causes a man to lust by the manner in which she is dressed (or undressed!) then she is an equal party. She has committed adultery in her heart, as well.

This is a quote from Dr. Hyles' sermon, "Mini-skirts In Light Of The Bible": "Did you know that for you to appeal to a man through the over-exposure of your body is a short-cut to being appealing? Do you know what appeals to a man? That sweet mystery about a woman. And when you just all of a sudden uncover everything and try to appeal to a man strictly through his physical senses, you're taking a short-cut to appealing to a man that overlooks the way you ought to appeal to him. The Bible says a meek and quiet spirit; that sweet mystery about a woman's personality. I think you ought to be pretty, and I think you ought to be attractive. It's a way of getting attention. But to expose your body for attention is a way of getting attention and notoriety without earning it. Anybody can get attention by taking off her clothes, but it takes a real lady to get attention through the sweet mystique of femininity." That's the opinion, not only of a great preacher, but of a man who knows how men are affected by the exposure of a woman's body.

What about the upper part of the body, the chest, the bust, the shoulders? Where does the Bible stand on styles that are low-cut, halter tops, sun-dresses, etc.? There is no question that the trunk, the main portion of the body, is to be covered. In Genesis 2 we find Adam and Eve, man and wife, in a state of innocence. They knew no sin, they had no sinful nature or wrong desires. When they did sin, and they lost their innocence, they immediately saw their need for clothing. *"And the eyes of them both were opened, and they knew that they were naked; and they sewed fig leaves together, and made themselves aprons."*

Even in their sinful state, they realized the need

for covering. So their human logic decided that they
would make aprons out of fig leaves. When God
entered the scene He provided them with 'coats of
skins'. I realize that this points to the difference
between a man-made righteousness, and the shedding
of innocent blood for our sins, but I'm not pointing out
the difference between the fig leaves and animal
skins. I want you to notice the difference between
aprons and coats.

Have you stopped to consider what an apron
covers? Not much! The Hebrew word signifies a
covering for the loins, maybe like the loin-cloth of
heathen cultures. (It probably covered more than
what is worn by people on the beach.) Adam and Eve
at their worst spiritual state felt the need for some
covering. But what they felt was enough covering to
suit a sinful man, did not cover enough to suit a holy
God. He made them coats of skins. What does a coat
cover? Considerably more than an apron, we can be
sure! Probably the same amount of the body that
would be covered by a robe. The main torso of the
body and the thighs.

Stop to think for a moment that Adam and Eve
were still alone in the Garden. There were no other
men to lust after Eve if she went to the grocery store.
The only Person who came to visit them was God. But
God wanted them to be sufficiently clothed and to be
modest in order to fellowship with Him. Does that
mean, then, that God considers modest apparel to be
important to our walk with Him? I think that it does.

We have a holy God who can't fellowship with sin.
He paid the Ultimate Price and gave His Son to die in

our place so that our sin could be paid for and we could once again fellowship with Him. The whole reason for separation in every area of our lives in not so we can glory in how good we are and what we don't do. The purpose is to clean up our lives from everything that is offensive to a holy God so that we can fellowship with Him and enjoy the walking and talking with Him that Adam and Eve once knew in the garden of Eden.

"Wherefore come out from among them, and be ye separate, saith the Lord, and touch not the unclean thing; and I will receive you, And will be a Father unto you, and ye shall be my sons and daughters, saith the Lord Almighty." (II Corinthians 6:17-18) God bids us to 'come out from among them', rather than 'go out from among them', because to separate from the world is necessary to separate TO God.

But it's senseless to separate from sin, and not go on to the sweet fellowship and walk with God that separation makes possible. Separation from the world without separation unto God is like the children of Israel stranded in the Wilderness where they could not have the leeks and onions of Egypt, nor could they enjoy the milk and honey of Canaan. That's like getting a daily ration of dirty laundry, dirty dishes and dirty house without getting a family to enjoy. In other words, that's DUMB. The answer is not to drop Bible standards of separation, the answer is to cultivate a walk with God.

That's why some people have turned their backs on Bible standards to go back to the world. They saw

Bible standards as only a needless burden, instead of a path to get further from sin AND closer to God. We need to see that Christianity is not summed up in the words, "Thou shalt not...", and realize that God wants us to leave behind something tainted and substandard, so that He can give us something far more wonderful and satisfying spiritually. Don't get stranded in the wilderness, but follow through with separation from the world AND separation unto God.

Two ladies somehow got into a conversation about the vast differences in their lifestyles though both of them were saved. One of them was a godly Christian who was separated from the world and lived and dressed in accordance with the Bible. The other lady clearly wore the mark of worldliness, and it was evident in her apparel, her entertainment, and every area of her life. She had everything she thought she wanted, yet she was extremely unhappy, and she envied the peace and contentment that she saw expressed in the life of this other lady. After they had talked awhile she said, "You know, I'd give the whole world to have the peace and contentment and happiness that you seem to have." The surprising reply was this: "Funny thing. That's exactly what it cost me."

What In The World Should I Wear? I should wear only that which is modest and loose-fitting, only that which covers the torso and thigh, only that which is clearly and distinctively feminine --- only that which fits God's rule of a 'long, flowing garment'. Don't let style, or peer pressure, or convenience, or the money that you've invested in a worldly wardrobe, or a spirit of rebellion keep you from obeying God in this matter. If the world offers a style that is within the Bible guidelines of a *katastole,* then we can enjoy wearing that style of clothing as 'using and not abusing' the world. The primary concern is that we do what will please the Lord.

When we began this study I challenged you to pray and promise God that whatever you saw in the Bible that was not a man-made rule, but really what God wanted in the area of ladies' dress, that you would obey Him. Now is the time to remember that promise, and follow through with some specific decisions and changes. I hope that I've been able to clearly present to you what the Holy Spirit and my good husband patiently taught me from the Bible about this matter in years gone by, and to answer this question for you: What In The World Should I Wear?

Please Excuse My Excuses...

Q. Aren't pants more modest for some activities than a dress?
A. No, they're not. God didn't just intend to hide the skin. The purpose of modest apparel is to conceal the feminine contours of a woman's body that appeal to a man, which are vividly displayed in pants.

Q. Isn't it too inconvenient and uncomfortable to wear dresses all the time?
A. First of all, convenience and comfort are not to be the determining factors for what we do. We ought to

base our decisions on right and wrong. Besides that, you feel comfortable in the clothes that you have worn the most. When you decide to wear only dresses and skirts, and modest, loose-fitting culottes, then that will become 'comfortable' to you, and in time you won't be able to imagine feeling comfortable in pants anymore.

Q. Isn't it 'legalism' to have rules and regulations for how you dress?
A. 'Legalism' means to add to the plan of salvation. If I were telling you that you have to wear a dress to be saved, then I'd be a legalist. But that is not what I'm saying. Jesus said, "If you love me, keep my commandments." If I really love the Lord, I'll want to please Him. This is merely a Bible study on what it means to please and obey the Lord in the area of dress standards. If you believe a woman ought to wear some kind of clothing in order to appear in public, then you have dress standards. The difference is that you got your standards from the world, and we adopted the standards of the Bible.

Q. If I require my daughter to dress according to the Bible, won't that make her rebel?
A. No, not any more than a rule against candy will give you cavities. It is the wrong dress practices, not scriptural dress practices, that promote rebellion and sin. What we do need to do is teach them WHY we have dress standards, show them what the Bible says, and encourage them to obey God because they want to please Him, not just because mom and dad say they

have to. Before you respond to rebellion by removing the obligation to do right, why not try removing the influence to do wrong, instead. Perhaps you're dealing with a situation of a teenager who has been allowed to dress improperly for years, and suddenly you're ready to make a change. Right is still right, and God blesses our obedience. But I would approach this with as much prayer as I would invest in the most crucial decisions in life, and beg God to make changes in the heart to match the changes that we are requiring outwardly.

Q. Isn't it 'unscriptural' to use Deuteronomy 22:5 as an argument against women wearing men's clothing, since some things mentioned in that chapter deal with ceremonial laws rather than moral laws?
A. NO! The favorite thing to do, if you don't want to obey a command in the Bible is to relegate it to ceremonial law or another dispensation. In the case of Deuteronomy 22:5, people have said that the command is invalid because verse 9 prohibits sowing different kinds of seed together, verse 10 prohibits plowing with an ox and ass together, and verse 11 prohibits wearing garments made of different materials. These *were* ceremonial laws which carried a spiritual significance or teaching. The ceremonial laws were all done away with when Jesus died and provided the true form of what these 'pictures' represented.

However, the same people who say that the command for distinction between male and female clothing is invalid for us today, never mention that

What In The World Should I Wear?

verses 1-4 deal with laziness and selfishness, verse 6-8 deal with our obligation to protect life, verses 13-30 deal with sexual trespasses such as adultery, rape, and incest. Are these issues also dealing with ceremonial law just because they appear in the same chapter with a command not to mix different types of material in one garment? Does that mean that these acts are now acceptable? They could just as easily be considered part of the context of ceremonial law as verse 5 which states that a woman shall not wear that which pertaineth to a man, yet I've never once heard that argument used to justify adultery, rape or incest. The contextual critics, for some reason, never seem to notice those verses.

The second reason I am sure that this is NOT a ceremonial law is because it is labeled an abomination. Some of the most wicked acts imaginable are called an abomination. Homosexuality, bestiality, incest, idolatry and blasphemous acts are referred to in scripture as 'abomination' AND men and women wearing the apparel that belongs to the opposite sex.